CELEBRITY ACTIVISTS™

AL GORE AND GLOBAL WARMING

ROSEN
PUBLISHING®
New York

DANIEL E. HARMON

Published in 2009 by The Rosen Publishing Group, Inc.
29 East 21st Street, New York, NY 10010

Library of Congress Cataloging-in-Publication Data

Harmon, Daniel E.
Al Gore and global warming / Daniel E. Harmon.—1st ed.
    p. cm.—(Celebrity activists)
Includes bibliographical references and index.
ISBN-13: 978-1-4042-1761-4 (library binding)
1. Gore, Albert, 1948– —Juvenile literature. 2. Legislators—United
States—Biography—Juvenile literature. 3. United States. Congress.
Senate—Biography—Juvenile literature. 4. Vice-presidents—United
States—Biography—Juvenile literature. 5. Environmentalists—
United States—Biography—Juvenile literature. 6. Global warming—
Juvenile literature. 7. Environmental policy—United States—History—
20th century—Juvenile literature. 8. Environmental policy—United
States—History—21st century—Juvenile literature. I. Title.
E840.8.G65H27 2008
973.929092—dc22
[B]
                                                    2007042977

On the cover: Inset: Al Gore. Background: This Live Earth concert took place on July 7, 2007, in Hamburg, Germany. Gore launched a series of concerts worldwide that took place over a 24-hour period to help combat global warming.

CONTENTS

INTRODUCTION

To Al Gore, the scene is both awesome and alarming. The front of an ancient glacier towers hundreds of feet above the ocean surface—a breathtaking sight to cruise excursionists off Alaska's coast. Sheer ice, the glacier's core is thousands of years old. One of nature's most magnificent spectacles, it may also be among the fastest-disappearing. News videos and science documentaries show astonishing collapses of these massive glacial fronts. In a movement called calving, tons of ice, loosened from the main glacier by melting, crash into the sea.

Half a world away off the Norwegian coast, a mother polar bear and her cub

Al Gore waves during a press conference in Hong Kong in 2006 to promote his documentary, *An Inconvenient Truth*. The film won an Academy Award.

stand at the edge of a melting ice floe. The mother growls and looks skyward, as if lamenting the loss of her frozen habitat. Scientists report that some polar bears in recent years have drowned because they have to swim farther to get from one ice floe to another. A twenty-year U.S. Geological Survey study in northern Alaska shows that pregnant female polar bears now tend to make birthing dens on land. In the past, they dug dens on floating ice, which remained frozen year in and year out.

Gore believes these are signs of the climate trend called global warming. To him, they are not just sad and disturbing; they tell of a planet in trouble. Global warming, he warns, is a "planetary emergency." Gore is convinced civilization has caused the crisis as a result of the Industrial Age of the past two centuries. And humans, he says, can solve the problem—if we act now.

In his 2006 book, *An Inconvenient Truth*, Gore surmises that "the truth about the climate crisis is an inconvenient one that means we are going to have to change the way we live our lives." Some changes will be relatively minor—adjusting our thermostats to cooler temperatures in winter and warmer temperatures in summer. Others will require major initiatives to switch from oil- and coal-based energy sources to less-polluting alternatives and renewable fuels (water, solar, and wind power).

If we fail to correct the problem, Gore predicts, catastrophe will result. The warming trend is developing at an accelerated pace—faster than researchers initially suspected.

The polar bear is just one of the animal species scientists believe are already in jeopardy because of global warming and the resulting loss of habitat. Other animals include certain whales, seals, and penguins; a variety of water birds; and tree frogs and golden toads.

Some scientists say that if we cannot control and reverse the warming phenomenon, human existence will be threatened, too. The Inuit people in parts of the Canadian Arctic are an early example. They travel over the ice to hunt for a living. In 2006, thinning ice made their traditional routes hazardous. This made it harder for them to obtain food.

Meteorologists suspect a warming climate is causing strong storms and bizarre weather patterns around the world. If freshwater rivers and lakes dry up as a result of droughts, people in many areas will find it difficult to obtain their most vital requirement for life: drinking water. The world's food supply, already of great concern to economists, likewise is in danger. Obviously, water shortages affect farmers' ability to produce crops.

Melting polar and glacial ice is causing sea levels to rise, erasing beaches and undermining coastal structures. It adds great volumes of freshwater to the

A female polar bear and her cub ponder a course from their floating iceberg. Unusual melting of polar ice has begun to create problems for humans as well as animals.

ocean, significantly changing the salty composition. This affects ocean life, including tiny plankton, which provide food for larger aquatic creatures and help convert carbon dioxide into oxygen. A break in the food chain can be ruinous.

Since life-forms are interconnected, warmer temperatures pose widespread complications and problems for all life on the planet, not just that which lives in or near the oceans. The warming of the air around us may feel like a pleasant change to people who live in cold regions. Elsewhere, though, it poses discomforts and health threats.

While humans evaluate the apparent changes in weather and climate, some animals, such as the polar bears, are already being forced to change their age-old patterns of existence. Another Arctic species endangered by warming is the Porcupine caribou. Warmer winters have changed the thaw-and-freeze action of the ground's surface, making it difficult on some days for the caribou to feed on lichen. Scientists think this kind of change could help explain why the Porcupine caribou population, estimated at almost 180,000 in 1989, has been reduced by a third in less than twenty years.

In the Andes of South America, atmospheric warming affects the moisture that is vital for plant growth and, consequently, for animal survival. Plant and animal species there are being forced to shift to greater heights to find necessary moisture. Such an adjustment for plant life takes decades or centuries. Certain species, scientists fear, won't have time to keep up with the warming trend and will become extinct.

Gradually rising atmospheric temperatures in other parts of the world have altered the migratory and residential patterns of birds, insects, and mammals. One example is the mockingbird; it was once rarely seen outside the American South, but now it lives in New England as well. Other birds no longer need to migrate with the changing seasons as they once did.

Insects, too, are experiencing changes in their habitation. Mosquitoes—which can carry malaria and other diseases harmful to humans—may expand their range and carry health threats to new human populations.

Since Al Gore's departure from public office in 2001, the former vice president of the United States, senator, and congressman has devoted much of his time to warning the world of alarming climate changes. The message is highly disturbing, but Gore delivers it in his patient southern drawl, assuring audiences that the problem is not beyond solution. His award-winning efforts have helped focus growing attention on global warming. In the process, they have made Gore a more prominent public figure today than ever before. Some observers believe he will be unable to resist a return to politics.

CHAPTER ONE

Son of a Statesman

When he was a child, Al Gore had no dreams of becoming an activist—for the environment or anything else—although he thought he someday might enter public service. His father, Albert Gore, whom the lad always considered a champion of just causes, was a progressive-minded politician. But young Al had many other things to command his attention from day to day. His was an unusual upbringing.

City Boy, Farm Boy

Albert Arnold Gore Jr. was born on March 31, 1948, in Washington, D.C. Both his parents were lawyers. At the

Senator Al Gore Sr. and his family leave the Capitol in Washington, D.C., in 1957. Al Jr. is at the far right; his mother, Pauline, is at the far left; and his sister, Nancy, is between the parents.

time, his father was a U.S. congressman from Tennessee. His mother, Pauline LaFon Gore, was a noted political thinker who helped her husband closely with his work on policy matters in Congress. She served as a member of his Washington staff and later became a delegate to the United Nations.

Congressman Gore, who became a senator in 1952, was a Democrat who sometimes took unpopular positions on social issues. Unlike most lawmakers from the South in the mid-1900s, he was a staunch supporter of civil rights and school desegregation. At the same time, he looked for ways to better the lives of all Americans. He was a leading supporter of the interstate highway system during the 1950s and an early advocate of Medicare. In *An Inconvenient Truth*, Al remembers his father as "a strong and courageous man with vision and integrity."

Even while Al was too young to understand anything of politics, the elder Gore was expressing a concern for the environment. Being a farmer, he was especially worried about over-cropping and other threats to the health of the soil. History had shown, he pointed out, that soil mismanagement could lead to widespread starvation. At the same time, Gore Sr. saw a close link between ecology and economics. As noted in Bob Zelnick's book *Gore: A Political Life*, Gore Sr. once wrote that although environmental preservation efforts "are noble goals, they are not the noblest: the noblest is to provide man with the basic stuff of his existence—food and housing, and meaningful work."

Pauline Gore was influenced strongly by Rachel Carson's pollution warnings in the acclaimed 1962 book *Silent Spring*. Pauline taught her children to be concerned about the environment. When Al was fourteen, his mother spent some of their evenings reading aloud from the book to him and his sister, Nancy. Nancy Gore was ten years older than Al. He recalls her lovingly as both his playmate and protector.

The family lived most of each year at the Fairfax Hotel, located in the embassy district of the nation's capital. They spent summers at their 250-acre (1,011,714 square meters) farm in the hills near Carthage, Tennessee. They raised cattle, tobacco, and other crops along the banks of the Caney Fork River. Although the boy was intrigued by the life and culture in Washington and received an excellent education at St. Albans School for Boys there, his

Author and biologist Rachel Carson stirred public interest in environmental concerns with her 1962 book, *Silent Spring*. The book deeply impressed Al Gore's mother.

heart was on the farm. He couldn't wait to return to Tennessee at the beginning of each summer.

The Gore farm was a wonderful place for a boy, with animals, canoes, and lots of space to roam. But it was a working farm, too, and Al had chores to do. His father taught him the importance of caring for the land, showing him simple techniques for preventing erosion.

In retrospect, Gore believes, his dual upbringing heightened his interest in nature. "Had I grown up entirely on the farm," he writes in *An Inconvenient Truth*, "I think I might well have taken nature much more for granted. But being deprived of it at the end of each summer allowed me to know it by its absence and to better appreciate its incomparable grace."

Al was an excellent student throughout grade school. According to Zelnick's *Gore: A Political Life*, a second grade teacher remembered, "[Al was] so mature and advanced I had to almost look at him to see whether he was a child or a man." During his senior year at St. Albans, Al was named a National Merit Scholarship finalist.

He was both mentally inquisitive and physically active. He lettered in basketball, football, and track.

Tobacco: A Family Dilemma

Part of the income from the Gore family farm near Carthage, Tennessee, came from growing tobacco. It was an important crop throughout the South for generations, and farmers such as Albert Gore Sr. were unashamed to produce it. In fact, until the 1970s, smoking was glamorized in broadcast and print advertisements. It was considered a suave, sexy habit—in spite of warnings by scientists and the U.S. surgeon general that it was a deadly health risk.

Al Gore's sister, Nancy, began smoking at age thirteen. She died of lung cancer in 1984 while only in her mid-forties. Her illness forced the family to question its tobacco production. Soon after her death, they stopped growing it.

During his first campaign for the presidency in 1988, Gore posed at the family farm near Carthage, Tennessee. The family by then had stopped growing tobacco.

He especially enjoyed writing and painting. Al even dabbled in teenage politics and was selected leader of the Liberal Party in his senior government class.

So varied were his interests, he was uncertain which academic path to take in college. Government? Literature? Naturally, he knew a great deal about agriculture, having spent much of his life as a farm boy. The farm, though, was mainly a retreat to him, not a likely vocation.

Eventually, Al would become highly successful as both a public servant and writer. And the Carthage farm would always be his retreat.

An Early Prophet of Global Warming

By the time of his high school graduation, Al had decided to pursue a career in writing. Entering Harvard University in 1965, he majored in English. Later, he changed his major to government. His education in those areas was important to his future work. It was a natural sciences class taught by Professor Roger Revelle, however, that brought the issue of Earth's climate to his attention.

Revelle not only taught science, he was also a pioneering scientist. During the 1950s, Revelle was

Sampling Politics

The old saying "Like father, like son" applied to Al Gore during his high school and college years. He deeply respected his father, a longtime congress-man who was elected to the U.S. Senate when Al was four years old. "As a boy," he recalls in *An Inconvenient Truth*, "I thought: why wouldn't I want to be like him?"

Al Gore Jr. was active in the Liberal Party at St. Albans, his Washington preparatory school. During his first year at Harvard University, he ran for fresh-man council. Although he had always been interested in becoming a professional writer, he eventually declared his major in American govern-ment at Harvard. He wrote his senior honors thesis about the changes television had caused in the functioning of modern presidents. Because of his father's position, he was able to interview some of the country's most famous political journalists in conducting his research.

By the end of 1970, though, the younger Gore had become disillusioned with politics. Negative cam-paigning had become the norm. Disappointed bitterly by his father's loss in the U.S. Senate race that year, Gore says in *An Inconvenient Truth*, he decided, "Politics would be the very last thing I did with my life." Six years later, however, he would reconsider.

the first scientist to propose studying the levels of carbon dioxide (CO_2) in the atmosphere. He recognized that during the economic boom and population explosion of the late 1940s and early 1950s, people were using much more petroleum and coal than in the past. They were putting more carbon dioxide into the atmosphere. What might this mean, in terms of atmospheric change? Revelle was determined to find out.

During the International Geophysical Year, which began in 1957, Revelle and an associate, Charles David Keeling, set up a research base atop Mauna Loa, a soaring volcanic mountain in Hawaii. Using weather balloons and other methods over a period of years, they collected air samples from high altitudes and analyzed the CO_2 content. Revelle understood that carbon dioxide buildup was occurring not just in the atmosphere, but also in the seas.

Later, as a Harvard professor, he told his students about his findings. Gore was riveted to Revelle's blackboard graphs showing the unmistakable rise in atmospheric CO_2 over time. He was also impressed by the professor's sincere concern. In *An Inconvenient Truth*, Gore writes, "He knew that this path our

Dr. Roger Revelle first drew Al Gore's attention to global climate problems while Gore was a student at Harvard. Revelle had discovered alarming increases in atmospheric carbon dioxide.

civilization had taken would send us careening toward catastrophe, unless the trend could be reversed."

Actually, scientists believe carbon dioxide in Earth's atmosphere began to increase long before World War II (1939–1945). They cite the Industrial Revolution of the 1700s and 1800s as the turning point toward environmental crisis.

The reason CO_2 in the atmosphere attracted little attention, even among scientists, until the mid-twentieth century is that it is barely measurable. In 1958, the average concentration of carbon dioxide in the air was found to be 316 parts per million (ppm) by volume. Forty years later, the average was 369 ppm. That is a tiny, tiny fraction of atmospheric content. But it has major significance. Analysts believe that before the Industrial Age, the carbon dioxide concentration was only about 280 ppm by volume. The fact that carbon dioxide content in our atmosphere is almost a third more than it was two centuries ago indicates an extremely rapid change.

In 1979, when Gore was a U.S. congressman, he invited Revelle to testify at a hearing on global warming. To his surprise, Gore says, Revelle's findings made little impression on other representatives.

Time has proved Revelle correct. Long-term studies now indicate the twentieth century was the hottest century since the Middle Ages. More alarmingly, since 1980, humans have experienced nineteen of the twenty warmest years since records have been kept.

Revelle died in 1991. Gore today praises him as a hero, and he includes the scientist's early CO_2 charts in his global warming presentations.

CHAPTER TWO

Journalism and Politics

The Vietnam War (1959–1975), so divisive among the American people, was especially trouble-some for Al Gore. He and his father both opposed U.S. military involvement in Southeast Asia. But in spring 1969, as the younger Gore approached graduation from Harvard and entered the military draft pool, he was worried about Senator Gore's political career. His father's outspoken opposition to the war was not the popular view among his Tennessee constituents. The senator faced a difficult reelection bid the following year. If his son dodged the draft, it could worsen the statesman's reelection chance.

Gore served as an army journalist in Vietnam. He enlisted despite his opposition to the war, partly to avoid discrediting his father in an upcoming Senate reelection bid.

Both parents shied away from influencing their son. The decision as to military service, they felt, should be his alone, without interference.

After deliberating at length, Al Gore enlisted in the army. He did not want to hurt his father's reelection campaign. More important, though, he says he did not want to live the rest of his life wondering whether one of his Carthage friends had been sent to war in his place. With his advanced education, he was assigned not as a frontline soldier but as an army public information specialist. After completing basic training in spring 1970, he was stationed at Fort Rucker in Alabama.

Beginning Life on His Own

While serving as an army journalist, Gore began planning his future career—and his future family. Between basic training and his active duty assignment, he married Mary Elizabeth "Tipper" Aitcheson. They had met at a high school dance in Washington, D.C., and had become engaged while in college. Tipper had been a student activist against the Vietnam War and later would become heavily involved in various social causes. (She has become well-known for her programs supporting mentally troubled children and the homeless, and for her 1980s campaign to have the music industry label recordings that contain violent and sexually explicit lyrics.)

The newlyweds spent weekends campaigning for Gore's father in Tennessee. Their efforts went for nothing; the senator was defeated by Republican William Brock in the bitterly fought 1970 Senate race. His father was "defeated by the politics of fear," Gore wrote in his 2007 book, *The Assault on Reason.* Many Tennesseans, he believes, questioned the senior Gore's patriotism because of his opposition to American involvement in Vietnam. Less than two months after the election, on Christmas Day 1970, the younger Gore was sent to Vietnam.

Covering the war as an army reporter was a harrowing experience. Gore witnessed the unwinnable plight of American soldiers—cast into a scenario in which their foes, the North Vietnamese, were often mistaken for their allies, the South Vietnamese soldiers. American forces resorted to unusual tactics, such as clearing jungle foliage with a chemical called Agent Orange. It deprived enemy guerrilla units of some of their hiding places, but it also deprived the land of millions of acres of greenery. For Gore, here was a graphic example of the conflict between humans and the environment.

Gore returned from Vietnam after eight months and completed his military service in 1971, still not knowing what career to pursue. Although his father's political record had always inspired him, he was disenchanted with politics as a solution to problems. He and Tipper settled in Carthage at the family farm. Gore worked briefly in home construction, then entered Vanderbilt University Divinity School in Nashville. While there, he got a job as a reporter for the *Tennessean* in Nashville. Tipper also went to work for the *Tennessean* as a photographer.

In 1974, while working for the newspaper, Gore switched from the divinity program to law school at Vanderbilt. Two years later, however, he decided not to become a lawyer. Friends urged him to enter the race for the middle Tennessee congressional seat being vacated by a retiring lawmaker. After years of ignoring the call, Al Gore followed his father into the political arena.

A Time of Protest

Beginning in the mid-1960s, public demonstrations against U.S. involvement in the Vietnam War were common in American cities and on college campuses. By 1970, protesters increasingly were voicing concern over environmental issues as well.

One infamous event in particular triggered environmental protest. The Cuyahoga River, flowing through the industrial district of northern Ohio, had become known as "the river that oozes" because of its thick, smelly oil content and floating debris. It was a convenient factory dump, carrying away toxic waste into Lake Erie. Pollution in the river was so bad that in 1969, it actually caught fire.

Most people had to admit that when a river caught fire, there was a serious problem. The debacle helped focus attention on pollution and prompted clean-up efforts. The first Earth Day was observed the following year.

During the 1970s, ecologists were preoccupied with the damage that pollution was causing to Earth's surface land and water. They also pressed for cleaner air to breathe. Automakers were required to control exhaust emissions, but most of the concern was localized, focusing on cities notorious for their smog. Few at the time were considering the global, climate-changing effects of air pollution.

A fireboat confronts an inferno floating on the Cuyahoga River near Cleveland in June 1969. Industrial waste dumped into the river fueled the fire.

Emerging Crises: Pollution and Energy

During the late 1960s and 1970s, Americans paid increasing attention to the environment. Public opinion polling in 1965 indicated that fewer than 20 percent of Americans viewed pollution as a major concern for the government. Just five years later, more than 50 percent considered pollution an important government issue. The first annual Earth Day in April 1970 heightened public awareness. Twenty million Americans, many of them college students, staged educational programs, debates, and demonstrations. Also in 1970, Congress established the U.S. Environmental Protection Agency (EPA).

Federal legislation was beginning to address environmental concerns. In 1899, Congress had passed the Rivers and Harbors Act, which banned certain forms of waste disposal. Subsequent laws included the Water Pollution Control Act of 1948, the Air Pollution Control Act of 1955, and the Air Quality Act of 1967. After 1970, new laws were added to give the EPA strong enforcement powers. They included the Clean Air Act (1970), the Clean Water Act (1972), the Safe Drinking Water Act (1974), the Resource Conservation and Recovery Act (1976), and the Toxic Substances Control Act (1976).

An important event occurred in 1973 that should have alerted Americans to a coming energy shortage, as well as to the ecological damage caused by the use of fossil fuels. In that year, Middle Eastern oil-producing nations reduced their shipments to the United States. Cars and trucks formed long lines at

Thousands gathered nationwide at the first Earth Day events in April 1970. These demonstrators in New York depicted the planet as a victim in dire need of help.

gas stations. Some stations went for days at a time with literally no gasoline to sell.

Americans were confronted with one aspect of what Al Gore would later call an "inconvenient truth." For the first time, they were forced to conserve energy, both on the road and at home. Some of the measures they were urged to take are identical to those that Gore and other environmentalists propose today:

- *Drive more fuel-efficient vehicles.*
- *Drive at moderate speeds.*
- *Set thermostats lower in winter, higher in summer.*
- *Insulate buildings properly.*
- *Reduce hot water usage.*

Innovators experimented with alternative power sources—solar, water, and wind. Federal lawmakers saw the obvious need to make the nation less dependent on fossil fuels. At the same time, legislators were increasingly concerned about pollution. They required automakers to produce vehicles that got better mileage and emitted less damaging exhaust into the atmosphere.

But the energy crisis soon passed. Americans renewed their preference for fuel-inefficient cars and trucks. In many households and offices, thermostats were returned to more comfortable but wasteful settings. A few progressive individuals still embraced solar power for heating homes and commercial buildings. By and large, though, people lost interest in developing alternative energy resources.

In his book *The Assault on Reason*, Gore states: "The energy crisis and the climate crisis are inextricably linked—both in their causes and in their solutions." He refers to "our civilization's tragic overdependence on burning massive quantities of carbon-based fuels."

Gore Goes to Congress

Gore wasn't expected to win his 1976 congressional race. He was only twenty-eight, and the closest claim he could make to having political experience was the investigative reporting and editorial writing he'd done for the *Tennessean*. Observers also believed his

Problems at the Pump

Drivers today complain about the high price of gasoline. For several weeks in 1973, drivers were happy just to be able to buy gas, at any price. Lines of vehicles in some places extended for blocks. Tensions flared. After waiting for many minutes, sometimes hours, motorists were limited to only a few gallons at a time. To keep the situation orderly, gas rationing was imposed. Drivers could buy gasoline only on certain days, depending on their vehicle license numbers.

What caused the crisis was a brief war between Israel and two Arab nations, Egypt and Syria. Oil-producing Arab countries cut back oil production and embargoed shipments to the United States, an Israeli ally. Although the cutback represented only a small percentage of world oil production, it was sufficient to create panic. After the crisis passed, Americans again were able to buy all the gas they wanted—at higher prices.

The silver lining in the dark cloud of the 1973 oil crisis was that it forced people—temporarily, at least—to examine alternatives to petroleum and other fossil fuels. They realized, too, that gasoline power is unfriendly to the environment. Such solutions as gasoline substitutes were cost-prohibitive, however. Gasoline remained the norm, carbon emissions

increased, and the greenhouse effect worsened. Still, the event gave Americans a preview of the "inconveniences" they must tolerate if they are to address the problem of global warming effectively.

Some drivers during the 1973 gasoline shortage had to wait in line for hours just to buy a few gallons of gas—and many stations languished for days with no gas to sell at all.

father's liberal voting legacy would hurt his election chances. But young Gore, taking moderate and even conservative positions on issues such as abortion funding and gun control, defeated eight other candidates in Tennessee's Democratic primary. This gave him the congressional seat, since the Republican Party was not competitively organized in the district.

During the months between his primary victory and taking office, Gore set about to prepare himself for Congress. The first thing he did was visit the Oak Ridge National Laboratory. The government research center in eastern Tennessee had been established by the army during World War II. Gore spent several days there gathering all the information he could about environmental and energy issues. "Even back then," he recalls in *An Inconvenient Truth*, "these were at the top of my list of priorities."

The seeds of interest planted by his mother, later nurtured by the ecological concerns of the early 1970s, would go with him to Washington.

CHAPTER THREE

The Global Greenhouse
Attracts Attention

Earth is a complex planet. All things are interrelated. One change in the routine life of a plant or animal species can affect many connected species. An alteration of a river flow or ocean current can impact whole food chains. The release of certain waste chemicals into the air, ground, or water can kill various life-forms and jeopardize secondary life-forms that are connected to them.

As Al Gore entered Congress, the lawmaking branch of government, his farm upbringing and college studies made him attentive to different areas of ecological concern that Congress might investigate. He wanted to see what could be done to control industrial waste and other forms of pollution. He wanted to explore the effects on humans of agricultural and industrial chemical use and disposal. In time, his interest began to focus on the big picture—the effects of human progress on Earth's atmosphere and what it might mean to the planet's future health.

What, Exactly, Is Up There?

Earth is enveloped by a layered atmosphere. Layers contain various gases, each of which has a role in the overall condition and livability of the planet. Carbon dioxide, vaporized water, and fluorocarbons are among the greenhouse gases that have come under increasing scrutiny since the 1980s. They are players in what has come to be known as Earth's greenhouse effect.

For ages and ages, heat rays from the sun have warmed Earth. Most of the heat, after serving its purpose, has escaped back into space. But this pattern seems to be going awry. Most scientists today believe Earth's surrounding atmospheric gases— which form a type of global "greenhouse"—have changed markedly during the past two centuries.

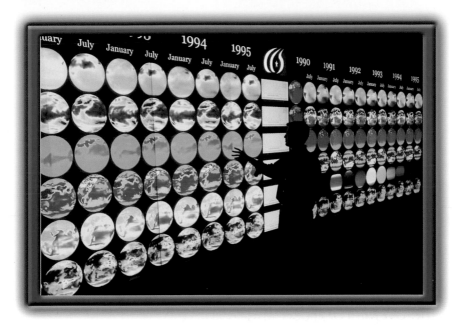

Scientists at the Oak Ridge National Laboratory in Tennessee have studied environmental data since World War II. Here, computerized images illustrate climate changes.

Many think the changes have been accelerating in the past quarter century. The effect, in a nutshell, is that an increasing volume of greenhouse gases in the atmosphere is preventing more and more of the sun's heat from returning to space. The greenhouse effect, scientists explain, produces global warming. With more heat being retained beneath the gas layers, the whole world gradually is becoming, literally, a warmer place.

The change was almost unnoticeable until the late twentieth century. Since the 1980s, Gore and others believe, it has progressed at an astonishing pace.

What is causing this atmospheric change? Primarily, the increase in human-generated air pollution, scientists say. Carbon dioxide emissions from automobiles and factories are the most often cited culprits.

The greenhouse effect matters because different life-forms on Earth depend on a very delicate balance of heat and coolness. A gradual change might not be noticeable to humans over a period of forty or fifty years, but plants and other animal species can be affected more quickly—and dramatically. What happens to them impacts other life-forms.

Warming also changes Earth's geological features. Particularly, scientists say, it is reducing the polar ice caps. This, as noted earlier, takes away local wildlife habitats while raising sea levels and changing the chemical composition of the oceans, which means a lot to ocean life-forms.

Carbon dioxide, one of the gases contained in the global greenhouse, is produced by the simple act of breathing. It's also produced by the burning of most energy resources—coal and oil for heating, and gasoline for automobiles. As more and more people inhabit the planet and produce more and more carbon dioxide, these gases are building up in the atmosphere. Among other results, they are altering the global heating equation.

What else is up there? Certain aerosol spray cans release fluorocarbons into the atmosphere. The rotting of household waste in landfills creates methane, another type of gas that makes up Earth's greenhouse.

American landfills are worse than smelly. Millions of tons of household waste eventually decay and create methane, a harmful greenhouse gas.

All of this pollution from automobiles and other forms of transportation, factories, garbage, and aerosol sprays adds gases to the "greenhouse layer" of the outer atmosphere. It thickens the layer and holds more heat inside the atmosphere and around Earth's surface. And that, Gore says—although changes may be only slightly noticeable from year to year or decade to decade—presents civilization with an acute survival problem.

Greenhouse Gases—What Are They?

Carbon dioxide is the gas that most concerns scientists who are worried about the greenhouse effect. It is not the only greenhouse gas, though. Others include ozone, methane, nitrous oxide, sulfur hexafluoride, and simple water vapor. These gases occur naturally and have affected Earth's climate from prehistoric times.

Earth's greenhouse blanket is very sensitive. A very slight variation in the amount of carbon dioxide in the atmosphere can cause overall temperatures to rise or fall. If the average temperature changes by just five degrees Fahrenheit (three degrees Celsius) or less over a period of a few decades, it can dramatically affect life on Earth.

But Is This Really "News"?

This is not exactly new "news." A few scientists began theorizing about global warming more than a century ago. Not until the 1950s, though, did atmospheric testing prove their suspicions correct— thanks largely to the work of Roger Revelle and his colleagues.

By 1983, the U.S. Environmental Protection Agency was alerting Americans to a global warming trend. In a report that year, the agency said world temperatures could rise by an average of several degrees Fahrenheit by the year 2100. If unchecked by that time, according to the EPA, the impact on civilization could be catastrophic.

At the time, many scientists were unsure of the overall meaning of surface temperature patterns. Temperatures had fluctuated up and down during the mid-1900s. Well into the 1970s, the trend seemed to be downward, not upward. Some scientists suggested the planet could be entering the next ice age. Ice— not heat.

In 2001, after more than a decade of research, the Intergovernmental Panel on Climate Change

(IPCC) reported that Earth's average atmospheric temperature had risen by 1 degree Fahrenheit (0.6 degree Celsius) since 1861. By the end of this century, the IPCC scientists predicted, the average temperature could rise approximately 2–10 degrees Fahrenheit (1.2–6 degrees Celsius) higher if greenhouse gas accumulations are not reduced. Even if they are, the warming trend could continue for another century or longer before the existing gases subside.

Until that sobering report was issued, relatively few people were seriously concerned about global warming. As Gore points out in his 1992 book, *Earth in the Balance*, they assumed "the earth's ecological system would somehow absorb whatever abuse we heaped upon it and save us from ourselves." Now, global warming is a regularly reported news category.

Legislating for the Environment

As a member of the Interstate and Foreign Commerce Committee in Congress, Gore participated in hearings into corporate misconduct. Many of the companies under scrutiny were involved in energy and environ-mental issues. Poisonous waste from industrial sites was a leading concern during the late 1970s and

A special issue of *Time* magazine in April 2006 probed different angles of the global warming problem. Abnormally melting polar ice is one of the warning signs.

early 1980s. In 1980, Gore was one of the sponsors of the Comprehensive Environmental Response, Compensation, and Liability Act. This legislation created a "Superfund" for the Environmental Protection Agency to use to clean up hazardous dump sites—at the expense of industrial dumpers.

Gore also pushed for stronger warning labels on cigarette packs. To some, his confrontation with the cigarette industry appeared hypocritical, for Gore's own family had profited from tobacco sales. The smoking debate came to be of special interest to Gore. His sister, Nancy Gore Hunger, a longtime smoker, died of lung cancer. His father afterward stopped growing tobacco, recognizing the health perils of smoking.

His sister died in July 1984, while Gore was campaigning for a U.S. Senate seat. He had decided to pursue the vacancy left by Tennessee's retiring senator Howard Baker. Though he was deeply distressed during the campaign, Gore won the election with surprising ease, in a year when Republicans generally fared well.

The environment continued to be among his top agenda items as a senator. In 1988, he flew to

Antarctica to gauge the effects of the 1970 Clean Air Act. He explored Brazilian rain forests the following year. Later, he visited other parts of the world, from the Arctic to central Asia, looking into the effects of environmental changes. He chaired the American delegation to the 1992 Earth Summit, a unique gathering of international heads of state to examine ecological matters.

Looking back, Gore says he repeatedly found that legislators and voters were little interested in

Factory emissions darken the sky and add pollutants to the greenhouse layer of Earth's atmosphere. Can they be reduced substantially without affecting the economies of industrialized nations?

the concept of planetary warming and its frightful significance. While a senator, he and others pushed legislation that would have limited carbon dioxide emissions; the measure failed.

In 1987, Gore announced his candidacy for U.S. president. He was only thirty-nine—one of the youngest presidential candidates in American history— and a freshman senator. One reason he entered the national race, he says, was to draw attention to the issue of global warming. But Americans still were unready to listen. In *An Inconvenient Truth*, Gore writes that he was unable to make it "a central focus in the American political dialogue."

During the Democratic primary campaign, Gore gathered support in his native South but encountered problems in other regions. After a dismal showing in the New York State primary, he dropped out of the race.

When Time Stood Still

Six-year-old Albert Gore, Al and Tipper's son, loved baseball. He was "happy as an oriole," so to speak, on April 3, 1989, when his parents and some friends took him to the Baltimore Orioles' opening game of the season. His energy couldn't be contained as they left the stadium. Bent on chasing a frolicsome friend, he pulled his hand loose from his father's grasp and dashed across a busy street—into the path of a car.

Al and Tipper Gore rushed to the still, broken form of their son lying beside the curb. He had been knocked 30 feet (9 meters) and slid 20 feet (6 m) more across the pavement. As they held him, crying and praying, two off-duty nurses who happened to be at the scene worked to keep the boy alive until an ambulance arrived. For those agonizing minutes— and the following three weeks, while they virtually lived at Albert's bedside at Johns Hopkins Hospital— time for the Gore family stood still. Both parents began to see their lives and purposes in a new light.

Gore describes the event in *An Inconvenient Truth* as "every parent's nightmare. I will never forget any part of it." Tipper Gore remembers that "every-thing else stopped" in their lives. The parents took turns staying with their son, day and night, in his hospital room.

Albert emerged at length in a full body cast. He'd suffered multiple broken bones and massive internal injuries. For almost a year, he could not use

Al Gore carries his son from the hospital after almost a month of treatment. The six-year-old was struck by a car in April 1989.

his right arm. In time, though, he made a complete recovery.

The accident, Gore says in *An Inconvenient Truth*, made him understand "what is really important . . . I asked myself how did I really want to spend my time on Earth? What really matters?"

Gore says the tragedy resulted in two personal pledges: to spend more time with his family and to focus his professional work on addressing what he considers "the climate crisis." It was during his son's rehabilitation that Gore began writing *Earth in the Balance: Ecology and the Human Spirit,* his first book. As he notes in *An Inconvenient Truth,* "The environment had, for years, been at the forefront of my policy concerns, but it had been competing for attention with a lot of other issues . . . I realized this was the crisis that loomed largest and should occupy the bulk of my efforts and ingenuity."

He began assembling a public media presentation and lecture (he calls it his "slide show") on atmospheric warming and its implications. Gore concluded that God had given him a second chance with Albert's life—and along with it "an obligation to pay attention to what matters and to do my part to protect and safeguard it."

CHAPTER FOUR

Vice President Gore

E*arth in the Balance*, published in 1992, sounded an urgent warning of climatic crisis. Global warming is only one of the topics Gore discusses in the book, though. He looks at a wide range of connected issues that he believes affect the worsening condition of Earth's atmosphere—and possible solutions. He considers different forms of pollution, the difficulties posed by the world's growing population, economics, and political foot-dragging.

In the book, Gore states that people need to "think strategically about our new relationship to the environment." His suggested plan for attacking the dilemma ranges from curbing population growth to developing technological solutions. He urges international cooperation and environmental education so people worldwide will understand the pending crisis.

Number Two in the Clinton Administration

After Bill Clinton secured the Democratic nomination for president during the 1992 primaries, he struggled with his selection of a running mate. He knew the coming campaign against incumbent president George H. W. Bush would be difficult. At length, Clinton narrowed down his original list of forty potential vice presidential candidates to one. He asked Al Gore to join him on the ticket.

Clinton's choice raised eyebrows among political analysts. Presidential nominees almost always look to bring diversity to their general election campaigns. Instead, Clinton had chosen a politician very much like himself. Both men were comparatively young, in their mid-forties. They both professed the Southern Baptist faith. More strikingly, to political observers, they were from adjoining states. In almost all presidential campaigns, nominees pick running mates from distant regions of the country, hoping to attract more voters.

Gore is pictured with President-Elect Bill Clinton and Clinton's daughter, Chelsea, after the 1992 election. As vice president, Gore took the lead in the Clinton administration's environmental policies.

Clinton and Gore won the November election, but with a minority of the popular vote. It was a three-candidate race that year. Independent contender Ross Perot made an unusually strong showing, receiving almost 20 percent of the ballots.

On taking office, President Clinton gave his vice president important leadership roles within the new administration. Gore became involved closely in America's delicate relations with its longtime Cold

War nemesis, Russia, and in the country's trade relations with neighboring Mexico and Canada. He was a leader in the progress of telecommunications, which was leading to the Internet phenomenon. And, as Clinton recognized, Gore was the logical member of the administration to champion the environmental cause.

Gore traveled to remote locales around the globe to see for himself the effects of climate change. As Gore says in *An Inconvenient Truth*, he made it a point to visit "hot spots where global warming has left its impact": Greenland, the Aral Sea, the Dead Sea, the Alaskan Arctic, New Zealand, the Nile and Congo rivers in Africa, the Galapagos Islands, and the Everglades in Florida. He also went to places where the planet's health was being dramatically wounded—the Chernobyl nuclear disaster site in Ukraine, for example.

What impressed him most was what he observed in Antarctica. The typical temperature there—58 degrees below 0 Fahrenheit (50 degrees below 0 Celsius)—is stunning to the uninitiated. But Gore learned that air pollution throughout history can be measured in Antarctica's ice cores. Scientists drill

From a helicopter in 1998, Vice President Al Gore views the Ukrainian power plant at Chernobyl. The worst nuclear accident in history occurred there twelve years earlier.

down into the ice and retrieve samples. They can determine which chemicals were present, and to what extent, at different points in time. "The ice," Gore says in the movie *An Inconvenient Truth*, "has stories to tell us."

Nations Unite to Help the Environment

The international community began working together on environmental issues in June 1992. One hundred and sixty countries sent representatives to the UN Conference on Environment and Development, called the Earth Summit, held in Brazil. They emerged with no binding agreement, but they drafted the United Nations Framework Convention on Climate Change. It stated the delegates' consensus that global warming was a potential crisis issue.

A more significant step was taken five years later at a conference in Kyoto, Japan. The Kyoto Protocol is an international environmental treaty. Countries that ratify the treaty agree to reduce their nationwide emissions of six different greenhouse gases, including carbon dioxide. Gore was involved in drafting the Kyoto Protocol. He tried unsuccessfully to persuade the U.S. Senate to ratify it. The ratification process began in 1997. Gore laments the fact that the United States is the only advanced nation that has not signed on. Some 141 other countries have.

The United States and China are the two countries that emit the highest volumes of carbon dioxide. Although China has ratified the Kyoto Protocol, the U.S. Senate unanimously voted against ratification because the treaty requires only industrialized

Activists demonstrate at the Asia-Pacific Economic Cooperation summit in Sydney, Australia, in September 2007. They urge support of the Kyoto Protocol for reducing greenhouse gas emissions.

nations to reduce CO_2 emissions. President George W. Bush, who took office in 2001, has expressed opposition to the treaty for the same reason.

Some scientists have recently begun wondering whether the Kyoto Protocol even matters. The global warming situation, they fear, may be worse than delegates to the Kyoto convention realized ten years ago. One scientist, Tim Flannery, observes in his 2005 book *The Weather Makers*, "Kyoto's target of reducing CO_2 emissions by 5.2 percent is little more than irrelevant . . . If we are to stabilize our climate, Kyoto's target needs to be strengthened twelve times over."

Gore himself in early 2007 called for a 90 percent reduction in CO_2 emissions in the United States by the middle of this century.

The Scientific Debate

During the 1990s, many scientists still questioned the reality of a global warming crisis. Some believed the computer models that were being developed to predict future temperature trends exaggerated the warming pattern and its potential effects on civilization. They required more data before they

Myths and Facts

Myth: Many scientists doubt that humans affect Earth's climate; it's only a group of alarmists who are creating the publicity.

Fact: Most scientists agree greenhouse gases produced by people are causing Earth to become warmer.

Myth: Since the climate always changes in cycles, we are probably experiencing just another cycle.

Fact: It's true that climate changes are cyclical, but modern levels of carbon dioxide emissions are historically abnormal.

Myth: By healing the hole in the ozone layer, we are solving the problem of global warming.

Fact: The ozone hole, a great concern during the 1980s and 1990s, has resulted in more ultraviolet radiation reaching Earth's surface from the sun. But this type of light isn't the primary cause of atmospheric warming.

Myth: Glacial melting is not widespread. In fact, Antarctic and other major ice sheets around the world are increasing, not melting.

Fact: Some ice sheets are growing, but overall, they are shrinking because of warmer temperatures.

Myth: Since temperatures in some parts of the world are not rising—and even seem to be dropping—it's inaccurate to speak of "global warming."

Fact: It's true some regions have experienced little change, but on the average, Earth's atmospheric temperature is increasing.

Myth: Global warming is good because winters will be less severe, which means we'll have to burn less heating fuel.

Fact: Although that's the case in certain areas, the negative effects of year-round warming far outweigh any savings in heating energy. Global warming is a complex phenomenon.

Myth: It's too late to correct the pattern of global warming.

Fact: "There are lots of things we can do—but we need to start now," according to Al Gore.

would be willing to sound an alarm. Most who did warn of global warming spoke of it as a calamity that could happen "someday." Only a handful urged immediate action.

Even if global warming was a trend and a cause for worry, the scientific community was unsure whether it resulted from human causes. Some, for example, proposed that sunspot cycles—far beyond human control—affect the temperature of Earth. Others suspected global warming is caused by the periodic weather phenomenon called El Niño. A warm Pacific Ocean current that circulates off the South American coast, El Niño generates a Pandora's box of weather problems, from droughts to severe storms.

Assuming a warming trend was in progress and was caused by humans, what should be done about it? Should severe restrictions be placed on carbon dioxide emissions? Should rain forest logging be banned? Should people wait for more information to tell them what to do? And, in the end, would effective solutions prove to be too costly for the world economy?

Meanwhile, scientists were divided over the possible long-term effects of global warming. Some warned that a worldwide disaster could occur within the span of a century. Others suggested any harmful effects would be felt only in specific regions, such as the Arctic.

A computer image in 1997 showed the extent of an El Niño system (white-and-red band) in the Pacific Ocean. The recurring warm-water mass disrupts normal weather patterns.

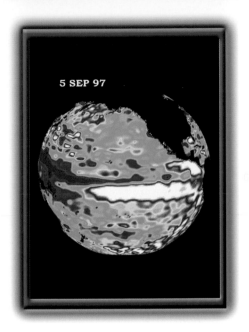

5 SEP 97

Gore contends now that the debate is essentially over. The great majority of researchers, he says, concur that global warming is a concern, that it is caused prima-rily by human activities, and that it is a real worldwide crisis. But during the years of his vice presidency, he was met with relatively little interest in the issue.

Presidential Candidate

Throughout his second term as vice president, many people assumed Gore would run for president in 2000. He did not make his public announcement until June 1999, but Gore had quietly begun laying the groundwork for his campaign soon after the

1996 elections were over. Not surprisingly, he embraced the environment as an important issue.

Other national concerns, however, were receiving more media coverage and largely shaped the 2000 election speeches and debates. They included universal health insurance, problems with the Social Security system, the fairest way to implement tax cuts, and public education. And Gore had to be extremely careful in depicting his ties to Clinton. Fresh in the minds of voters were Clinton's extra-marital affair and his impeachment on charges of obstructing justice and lying under oath to cover up the scandal. Gore had stood by Clinton faithfully during Clinton's political crisis. But he asserted in his campaign that as president, he would be his own man, not a Clinton clone.

Bill Bradley, a former U.S. senator from New Jersey, was Gore's main challenger in the Democratic primaries. Bradley and Gore largely agreed on basic issues, but Bradley contended that Gore was likely to lose the White House to a Republican candidate because of his long affiliation with the scandal-plagued Clinton administration. Nonetheless, Gore easily overpowered Bradley in the early Democratic primaries. Bradley's withdrawal from the race in March 2000 gave Gore eight months to focus his campaign against the Republicans.

George W. Bush won the Republican nomination and became Gore's chief rival for the presidency. In one of America's closest presidential elections, Gore narrowly won the popular vote, but he lost the electoral vote. The vote was so close in Florida that a gut-wrenching legal battle over recounts kept the final outcome in suspense for five weeks after election day. Gore finally conceded to Bush on December 13, 2000.

Some political analysts believe a minor candidate cost Gore the election. Ironically, the possible spoiler was a fervent champion of the environment. Ralph Nader, who received only 3 percent of the popular vote, represented the Green Party.

It will never be known how many Green Party supporters would have voted for Gore. Many Democratic leaders believe, though, that if Nader had not been a candidate, those voters would have given Gore the decisive state of Florida.

Though crushed, Gore accepted the defeat and refocused on his life's purpose. "This certainly wasn't an easy time," he wrote in *An Inconvenient Truth*, "but it did offer me the chance to make a fresh start—to step back and think about where I should direct my energies."

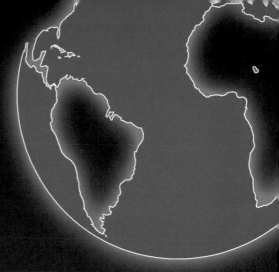

CHAPTER FIVE

Campaigning for a Healthier Planet

It was a challenging question. Where, indeed, should Al Gore direct his energies in the aftermath of his emotional 2000 election loss? For more than twelve years, he had had his political sights on the White House. Now, that dream seemed more unattainable than ever.

As time would prove, his great disappointment would bring Gore, in a sense, "down to earth" from the elevated heights of the presidential administration. It would reconnect him with the people.

During the United States' early decades, Americans discussed matters of importance at "town meetings." Today, the modern media feeds

Americans up-to-the-minute news on television as well as commentary on political and social developments. But the town meeting setting is still important for discussing local issues of concern.

Throughout his legislative career, Al Gore favored the town meeting as a forum for airing issues and answering questions. He understood the need to stay in close touch with his constituents. As a congressman and senator, he regularly returned home to Tennessee on weekends to meet with them, hear of their problems, answer their questions, and explain what he was doing in Washington. In all, during those years, he appeared at some 1,600 town meetings.

In the months after his razor-thin presidential election loss, Gore reevaluated his purpose in life. One of the first things he must do, he decided, was resurrect his "slide show" on global warming and take it directly to the people. Individuals needed to understand the looming crisis and start to take action. Urged on by his wife, Gore took to the road.

Global Warming On-Screen

Gore had given his first slide show on global warming at a Washington, D.C., dinner party in 1989, while

Since the beginning of his public service career, Gore has regularly returned to his home state to hear people's concerns and answer questions. His efforts have been greeted warmly.

serving in the Senate. At the time, it literally was a presentation of photographic slides. Today, Gore uses computer technology to display his visual message in large-screen format. Many weeks, he presents the show daily—sometimes more than once each day—to diverse audiences. Meanwhile, trained helpers are also presenting the show, multiplying its audiences worldwide.

In 2006, the essence of the slide show became available to everyone in the form of a book. "It was Tipper who first suggested that I put together a new kind of book with pictures and graphics to make the whole message easier to follow, combining many elements from my slide show with all of the new original material I have compiled over the last few years," he writes in *An Inconvenient Truth*.

Few who watch the documentary *An Inconvenient Truth* or read the heavily illustrated companion book can fail to miss the message. In a polite way, Gore is telling everyone to act—now—to avert a global catastrophe. The ultimate disaster may not occur during today's generation, but unless people immediately begin to change, climate warming can severely affect their children and grandchildren.

an**inconvenient**truth
A GLOBAL WARNING

SPECIAL FEATURES

Al Gore presents over 30 minutes of updated information.

Includes the **Melissa Etheridge** music video, "I Need to Wake Up."

Also includes things you can do to help.

A portion of the proceeds from the sale of this DVD will benefit the bipartisan climate effort, *The Alliance for Climate Protection.*

THIS LABEL IS MADE FROM NATURAL PRODUCTS 100% COMPOSTABLE

"It doesn't matter whether you're a Republican or Democrat, liberal or conservative... your mind will be changed in a nanosecond."
- Roger Friedman, *FOXNEWS.com*

Gore's documentary won an Academy Award in 2007. He was later commended by the Nobel Peace Prize committee for "efforts to build up and disseminate greater knowledge about man-made climate change."

Gore points to a variety of early evidence of damage from global warming. In balmy waters around the world, coral reefs are dying. Scientists cite different reasons, from harmful fishing practices to water pollution. But the leading culprit, they believe, is global warming. The ocean's average temperature has risen approximately 1 degree Fahrenheit (0.6 degree Celsius) during the past one hundred years, they say. This, combined with the effects of greenhouse gases on saltwater chemistry, has caused a form of bleaching and has weakened corals' process of creating and maintaining reefs. Meanwhile, more frequent and powerful storm systems, which may be caused by global warming, can destroy reefs.

Why should we worry about the loss of underwater reefs, which few people ever even see? Because a fourth of the sea's wildlife species rely on coral reefs as their main habitat. They include important commercial fish, as well as smaller life-forms on which the fish feed. In addition, reef systems help protect coastal areas from incoming hurricanes and tidal waves.

A *New York Times*/CBS News poll in spring 2007 questioned citizens on their opinions of global

The Great Barrier Reef off the Australian coast is a focus of study by scientists. Rising sea temperatures, they believe, damage reefs and affect the wildlife that depend on them.

warming, based on their political leanings. Nine out of ten Democrats, eight of ten independents, and six of ten Republicans said they believed the crisis called for immediate action. No one knows to what extent Gore's efforts have influenced public opinion. Since he's the public figure who is more closely identified with the issue than anyone else, however, virtually everyone credits Gore with having a great impact.

"Working Harder Than Ever"

Although retired from the Washington political scene, Gore is by no means retired. He may be busier today than at any point in his life. Most important, for the past six years he's been free to

What Are "Green Fuels"?

"The most vulnerable part of the earth's ecological system is the atmosphere—vulnerable because it's so thin," Gore explains in his documentary, *An Inconvenient Truth*. "And it's thin enough that we are capable of changing its composition."

Gasoline-powered vehicles are among the leading polluters of the atmosphere. What alternative fuel sources are available to help keep the planet "green"? Perhaps the following:

- **Diesel.** Even though it derives from oil, diesel for years has been considered a more environmentally friendly auto and truck fuel than regular gasoline. It runs "cleaner" (because of its low sulfur levels) and provides up to 40 percent better mileage.
- **Biodiesel.** This is a blend of oil-based diesel fuel with alternatives that include soybean oil. It emits only about a third as much greenhouse gas as regular gasoline.
- **Ethanol.** Ethyl alcohol, or ethanol, can be "brewed" similar to alcohol. Corn is a common source. Ethanol for some time has been blended with gasoline. However, ethanol fuel stations are hard to find outside the Midwest, where corn is a major farm crop. Developers are experimenting

with other types of plants and even with waste material as viable raw sources of ethanol. Skeptics wonder whether ethanol can be created economically or in large enough volumes to matter much in helping the environment.

- **Electric batteries.** Battery-fueled cars produce only about half the greenhouse emissions of gas-powered autos. A key problem is that electric-powered cars are expensive.
- **Natural gas.** While it runs cleaner than petroleum-based fuels, natural gas—like petroleum—is a dwindling natural resource.
- **Hydrogen.** Hydrogen as an automotive fuel can offer not only excellent mileage, but also the possibility of zero greenhouse gas emissions. To develop it as a marketable power source, though, auto manufacturers would need to invest formidable sums in research.

A switch to more Earth-friendly fuels not only could help correct global warming, it would also reduce personal health hazards. Much of the lower atmospheric pollution, including big-city smog, is caused by fossil fuel combustion.

devote his time and energy to the things in life that interest him most. Besides traveling the globe with his climate change message, he's involved in technology and media projects.

In keeping with his populist bent, Gore in 2005 cofounded Current TV, an interactive television news channel, with Joel Hyatt, a leading Democratic Party fund-raiser. The cable and satellite channel, which targets young adults, presents short video stories provided by viewers—"anyone with a camera, drive, and a story to tell," according to its statement of purpose. Gore sees it as a twenty-first-century method of empowering people. He explains in *An Inconvenient Truth* that "viewers themselves can make the programs and in the process participate in the public forum of American democracy."

Gore holds numerous leadership roles with businesses and environmental organizations, including Apple, Inc.; Google; the Alliance for Climate Protection; and Save Our Selves. In November 2007, he became a partner in a finance firm that supports start-up companies developing energy alternatives. He preaches his environmental message in boardrooms as well as in public. Gore persuaded Apple to phase out its use of toxic chemicals in its computer products by 2008.

Candidate Gore?

Gore, like many other environmentalists, has strongly criticized the Bush administration's environmental policies. They feel Bush is hopelessly indebted to the oil industry for his political support. As noted in *An Inconvenient Truth*, Gore says a handful of multinational companies are "spending many millions of dollars every year in figuring out ways of sowing public confusion about global warming."

The scientific community is by no means confused, Gore contends. In *The Assault on Reason*, he says: "There is no longer any credible basis for doubting that the earth's atmosphere is heating up because of global warming. Global warming is real. It is happening already, and the anticipated consequences are unacceptable."

Gore charges that Bush failed to honor his 2000 campaign promise to regulate carbon dioxide emissions in the United States. He contends that Bush has weakened or eliminated regulations that were in place before 2000 and that Bush favors large

Gore appears at a book signing in May 2007. In *The Assault on Reason*, Gore discusses the political environment today and how major issues are debated and decided.

corporate interests when it comes to protecting the environment. In *An Inconvenient Truth*, Gore states, "During the Clinton-Gore years we accomplished a lot in terms of environmental issues . . . Since the change in administrations, I have watched with growing concern as our forward progress has been almost completely reversed."

Some political observers expected Gore to make another run for the presidency in 2008. They believed the mounting publicity he has attracted with his global warming message would have enhanced his prospects of victory. Although he did not personally endorse them, a number of Web sites were established to organize support for a presidential campaign.

Gore insisted he would not be a candidate. "At first I thought I might run for president again," he says in *An Inconvenient Truth*, "but over the last several years I have discovered that there are other ways to serve, and that I am really enjoying them." Gore especially values "the satisfaction that can be found as a private citizen in trying to make our democracy work better."

In late 2007—after many candidates of both major parties had been campaigning for almost a year—he remained firm in his refusal. As reported in a May 16, 2007, *Time* article, Gore claimed he has "fallen out of love with politics." Still, some predicted he would make a belated entry into the Democratic primary campaigns.

Gore certainly views global warming as a political issue. But he thinks it is more than that. "Ultimately, this is really not a political issue so much as a moral issue," he states in the documentary. "If we allow [climate disaster] to happen, it is deeply unethical."

In *An Inconvenient Truth*, he describes a "coalition" of "powerful people and companies making enormous sums of money from activities they know full well will have to change dramatically in order to ensure this planet's livability." Those profiteers, he alleges, financially support politicians who vote in favor of their lobbying causes.

Gore discredits detractors who fear that saving the environment will weaken the world's economy. In the documentary *An Inconvenient Truth*, he says, "If we do the right thing, then we're going to create a lot of wealth and we're going to create a lot of jobs, because doing the right thing moves us forward."

Candidate or not, Gore has made it clear he will continue to press for action on the issue of global warming and will challenge those who stand in the way of a vigorous response.

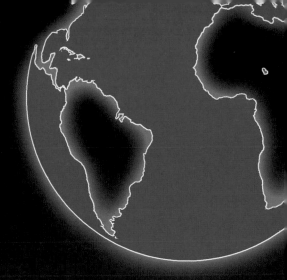

CHAPTER SIX

Signs, Skeptics, and Solutions

T he snowstorm was unusually heavy, burying Buffalo, New York, under 22 inches (56 centimeters) of cold whiteness in a single night. Buffalo's citizens are accustomed to snow and ice, but this event was different. It was mid-October 2006—very early in the season for a blizzard of such magnitude. Thirteen people died. Hundreds of thousands lost power for days. Trees still clad in their magnificent autumn colors cracked and collapsed under the snow's weight.

It was one of the numerous examples of weird weather that has been catching meteorologists off-guard in recent years. Analysts ultimately pinned the

The October 2006 snowstorm in New York State was remarkable for its early arrival and its severity—up to 2 feet (0.6 m) of snow in some areas.

blame on complex conditions in the atmosphere that altered the typical development of lake effect snow. But in the greater scheme of things, many scientists believe the overriding cause of recent weather anomalies is a rising global temperature.

Public Recognition

For his exhaustive research on such a complicated subject and his ability to explain it clearly to ordinary people, Gore has won prestigious awards. In 2006, he won a Quill Book Award for *An Inconvenient Truth*. The documentary won an Academy Award in 2007. Meanwhile, his Current TV project won a 2007 Emmy Award.

His crowning honor came in October 2007, when he won the Nobel Peace Prize for his global warming activism. The Nobel committee also bestowed the coveted award on the Intergovernmental Panel on Climate Change, the UN scientific network that has been studying climate patterns.

Gore's book *The Assault on Reason* was published earlier in 2007 and immediately attracted media and public attention. Within months of its release, it, too, won a Quill Book Award. *The Assault on Reason* is

Tipper Gore joins her husband at an October 2007 press conference in California. Gore had just been awarded the Nobel Peace Prize.

largely an attack on the Bush administration. Besides blocking the free exchange of information and trampling individual rights, Gore charges, the president is guilty of environmental neglect. He says Bush has ignored indisputable facts in formulating his policies concerning the environment and other issues. Gore notes that during his 2000 presidential campaign, Bush seemed genuinely concerned about global warming. However, this stance changed after the inauguration, Gore says.

Gore does not stop there. He faults the entertainment-focused media for their sensational presentation of information and says they are subject to political manipulation. Gore also takes the different branches of government to task for what he considers their complacency. He has pointed out in public appearances that America's governmental system has checks and balances and the country has a free press. Therefore, no one individual or group can bear the full blame.

Some reviewers seemed surprised by his tone in *The Assault on Reason*. They felt the book exposed an "angry" Al Gore, whereas his previous writings—although jolting—had been less shrill.

Opposing Voices

Almost from the beginning of his campaign to save the environment, Gore's motivations have been discussed. It's been suggested that he presumes to be more of an expert than he really is—an activist at times prone to "play shrink," in the words of Zelnick in *Gore: A Political Life*. Some have condemned him for profiting from the climate crisis by making himself a champion of the cause, although Gore donates all the earnings from *An Inconvenient Truth* to a nonprofit environmental policy organization.

Gore has also been criticized for exaggerating the problem of global warming and for using inappropriate examples to illustrate it. Some of the material he presented in *An Inconvenient Truth* was not fresh news—part of it long had been public knowledge. Part of what was new raised questions, in the minds of some.

In *An Inconvenient Truth*, Gore shows heartrending images of the indescribable tragedy of Hurricane Katrina in August 2005. He observes that Katrina was not a particularly destructive storm until it "passed over the unusually warm waters of the Gulf of Mexico." It then churned into the Gulf Coast as a category 3 hurricane, killed almost two thousand people, and rendered parts of New Orleans unlivable.

Critics point out that New Orleans was overdue to receive a catastrophic hurricane. Meteorologists had speculated about it for years, and the city obviously was unprepared. A category 5 hurricane, Camille, had devastated the Mississippi coast nearby in 1969.

Others wonder about Gore's suggestion that hurricanes now might be occurring more frequently and with greater force. It's true, as Gore notes, that 2005 was the most active hurricane season on record and that in 2004, for the first time in recorded history, a hurricane occurred in the South Atlantic. Comparatively few Atlantic hurricanes, however, developed in 2006 and 2007. Skeptics also assert that the main reason modern-day hurricanes are so destructive is not because they're that much stronger or frequent than those in the past. Rather, it's because of the massive construction along the Atlantic and Gulf coasts. Billions of dollars worth of seaside property is subject to direct hits. Some weather analysts seem surprised more damage and loss of life from hurricanes has not occurred.

The *Assault on Reason* was an instant best-seller, but it received mixed reviews. Many agreed with Gore's ideas, including his suggestion that it is the interactive Internet, not the entrenched news media, that can restore power to the people and better solve problems. "The Internet," Gore writes, "has the potential to revitalize the role played by the people in our constitutional framework." Critics, meanwhile, saw the book at least partly as a self-serving venture conceived to draw attention to its author as well as to its arguments.

Public service and public image unavoidably go hand in hand. Regardless of how he's perceived, Gore appears determined to continue pressing his message of the need for worldwide action to prevent a climate calamity.

More Than One Solution

Gore suggests many ways that society can reduce the trend of global warming. At the same time, he contends, we can improve our economy and overall quality of life.

Solutions proposed by Gore and others include finding new ways to harness more solar, water, and

What Individuals Can Do

Al Gore believes the climate crisis will be solved "only if we as individuals take responsibility for it." In *An Inconvenient Truth*, he suggests specific steps people can take to reduce global warming. Among them:

- Buy energy-efficient lighting and appliances; compact fluorescent lighting is one example.
- Use less hot water.
- Walk or bike, rather than drive, when possible.
- Drive slower (fuel economy decreases when driving faster than 55 mph [89 kilometers per hour]).
- Try to avoid rush-hour traffic.
- Consume less and buy items that last longer.
- Recycle, and buy products from manufacturers that use recycled packaging.
- Use paper only when necessary.
- Take along reusable tote bags when shopping.
- Eat less meat; meat production and transportation are energy-intensive.
- Buy local foods and other products when possible, reducing the need for product transportation.
- Plant trees.
- Learn about energy consumption and how individuals are wasting natural resources.
- Demand change from government leaders.

- Encourage your school to reduce carbon dioxide emissions.

  Energy conservation has added benefits, Gore points out. Walking and biking, rather than riding in cars and buses, improve our physical health. Using less electricity and fuel saves money.

One way to reduce fossil fuel consumption is to get around by bicycle when possible. Shown here is a "bicing" station— a shared bicycle service—in Barcelona, Spain.

wind power. Hydrogen fuel cells can power electric cars. More hybrid automobiles and buses can be made and marketed. More green space, including the roofs of building complexes, can be established.

Consumers can alter the marketplace by embracing such power-reduction items as compact fluorescent light bulbs. Utility companies can develop geothermal power stations.

Many Americans are taking personal initiatives to help the planet. So are small companies. Some are approaching the problem with an innovative spirit. For instance, researchers are working to perfect algae farms. Algae fats can be converted to biodiesel fuel, and algae help convert carbon dioxide to oxygen.

Even professional offices are joining the "green" movement, thanks in part to Gore's efforts. Inspired by

An Inconvenient Truth, the editor of a legal technology magazine initiated a regular "Green Law" feature. Legal professionals around the country

Turbine blades spin on a wind farm on Evia, an island off the Grecian coast. Wind—if it can be harnessed efficiently—is a clean and renewable energy source.

take turns describing how they are addressing the problem and encouraging others to do the same. Some law firms are committing to greater use of the Internet for video conferences, for example, which decreases travel requirements. By producing more of their letters and legal documents in electronic format only, they are trimming paper consumption.

Government agencies are beginning to see the advantages of "green" economics. Some city and town governments are partnering with fuel companies to buy alternative fuels for their fleets of emergency and administrative vehicles.

A few scientists have expressed doubt that people and governments will respond quickly enough to avoid disastrous consequences of global warming. Even if they try, scientists believe, ordinary measures may be insufficient. Some think even a heroic reduction in carbon emissions won't stop global warming. Radical—and risky—solutions might be necessary, they predict. One suggestion is to deliberately release more sulfur dioxide into the upper atmosphere. The effect would be to block a fraction of the sun's heat from penetrating the greenhouse layer—just enough to balance the overall warming trend.

Others theorize that a space-based solution is possible. A cluster of silicon disks launched into space between Earth and the sun, they think, can deflect some of the sun's heat before it reaches Earth's atmosphere.

Most researchers, however, urge practical steps to solve the problem. According to Gore, the United States can reduce pollution "to a point below 1970s levels" by:

- *Reducing U.S. consumption of energy for heating, cooling, lighting, and various electrical appliances*
- *Designing homes and other buildings that require less energy*
- *Buying more fuel-efficient autos, including hybrids and cars powered by fuel cells*
- *Designing better mass transit systems and more economical commercial hauling vehicles*
- *Relying more on renewable energy sources, including wind and biofuels*

- *Controlling carbon emissions more effectively at industrial and power production sites*

Statistics indicate the average American emits approximately 15,000 pounds (6,804 kilograms) of carbon dioxide each year, Gore notes. He believes American consumers gradually are turning away from "large, inefficient gas-guzzlers" and are looking for more fuel-efficient vehicles. Equally important, he sees a trend among corporate executives favoring clean environmental policies. They are beginning to understand that a planet-friendly approach to business is ultimately good for the economy.

Don't Panic. Do Take Action.

Al Gore's warning of an environmental crisis inevitably is one of gloom and possible doom. But his conclusion, as he writes in *An Inconvenient Truth*, is positive: "We can do something about this!"

People in the past have worked together to solve common problems, Gore says, and they can do so now. He points out that jointly, nations resolved the

Activists make a statement in giant letters at a Czech Republic coal mine. Gore and other environmentalists hope to build international support for their cause.

stratospheric ozone crisis from the mid-1980s to the mid-1990s. They did so largely by regulating the emission of chlorofluorocarbons (CFCs), commonly used for refrigeration.

Gore observes in *An Inconvenient Truth*: "Each one of us is a cause of global warming, but each of us can become part of the solution: in the decisions we make on what we buy, the amount of electricity we use, the cars we drive, and how we live our lives."

GLOSSARY

aerosol A spray product such as hair spray or air freshener that is released into the air by a gas propellant.

carbon dioxide (CO_2) A gas created by breathing and the breakdown of organic matter.

constituents Citizens of a specific voting district.

ecology The science of the relationship between living organisms and the environment.

electoral vote The official presidential vote cast by the 538 members of America's electoral college; the number of electors representing each state in the electoral college is the same as its number of U.S. senators and representatives.

environmentalist A person who works to protect Earth's environment from pollution, erosion, and other threats.

food chain The sequence in which one organism lives by feeding off of another.

fossil fuels Petroleum, coal, and other fuels that were formed by the remains of ancient living organisms.

greenhouse effect A warming of the climate caused by more of the sun's heat being trapped within Earth's atmosphere.

lobbyist A political worker who tries to influence legislation on behalf of a special-interest group.

meteorologist A scientist who studies weather changes caused by atmospheric activity.

methane A form of gas used as a fuel; also called marsh gas.

ozone A bluish, poisonous gas; the layer of ozone high above Earth protects the surface from ultraviolet sun rays.

populist A politician who identifies especially with rural and working classes.

ratify To accept the terms of a treaty.

smog The combination of smoke and fog that pollutes the lower atmosphere in some industrialized and densely populated areas.

treaty A formal agreement involving two or more countries.

FOR MORE INFORMATION

Climate Action Network Canada

412-1 Nicholas Street

Ottawa, ON K1N 7B7

Canada

(613) 241-4413

Web site: http://www.climateactionnetwork.ca

This network of Canadian organizations is "dedicated
to preventing dangerous levels of human interference with the global climate system, protecting
environmental sustainability and public health,
while upholding principles of just transition,
equity and social justice."

Current TV

118 King Street

San Francisco, CA 94107

(415) 995-8200

Web site: http://www.current.com

This peer-to-peer news and information network
allows you to share stories, news, videos, and
opinions on the Web. The independent media
company was cofounded by Al Gore.

Environment Canada

70 Crémazie Street

Gatineau, QC K1A 0H3

Canada

(819) 997-2800

Web site: http://www.ec.gc.ca

Environment Canada is the Canadian government's
   department that works to preserve natural
   resources, conserve renewable resources, and
   coordinate environmental policies with the federal
   government, among other activities. See especially
   the Green Lane at the department's Web site:
   http://www.ec.gc.ca/climate/home-e.html.

Intergovernmental Panel on Climate Change

IPCC WGI TSU

DSRC R/CSD8

325 Broadway

Boulder, CO 80305

(303) 497-5628

Web site: http://ipcc-wg1.ucar.edu

The panel studies information from scientists and other
   researchers to better understand climate change.

NASA Goddard Institute for Space Studies
8800 Greenbelt Road
Greenbelt, MD 20771
(301) 614-5634
Web site: http://www.giss.nasa.gov
The GISS is an Earth Sciences Division laboratory
at the National Aeronautics and Space
Administration's Goddard Space Flight Center
and is part of the Columbia University Earth
Institute. Much of its recent research has been
focused on climate change.

National Resources Defense Council
40 West 20th Street
New York, NY 10011
(212) 727-2700
Web site: http://www.nrdc.org
The mission of this environmental action group is
"to safeguard the Earth." Sections of its Web site
provide information and discussion on various
environmental issues, including global warming
(see http://www.nrdc.org/globalwarming/
default.asp).

National Wildlife Federation
11100 Wildlife Center Drive
Reston, VA 20190
(800) 822-9919
Web site: http://www.nwf.org
The federation's Web site devotes a section to global
warming: http://www.nwf.org/globalwarming.

Stop Global Warming
15332 Antioch Street, #168
Pacific Palisades, CA 90272
(310) 454-5726
Web site: http://www.stopglobalwarming.org
This is a nonpartisan "movement about change,
as individuals, as a country, and as a global
community."

U.S. Environmental Protection Agency
Ariel Rios Building
1200 Pennsylvania Avenue NW
Washington, DC 20460
Web site: http://www.epa.gov
The agency's Climate Change section suggests ideas
for reducing greenhouse gases.

The Weather Channel

300 Interstate North Parkway

Atlanta, GA 30339-2404

Web site: http://www.weather.com

The cable TV channel provides uninterrupted information on local, national, and international weather. Its Web site includes Forecast Earth (http://climate.weather.com), a section containing special information about global warming and related issues.

Web Sites

Due to the changing nature of Internet links, Rosen Publishing has developed an online list of Web sites related to the subject of this book. This site is updated regularly. Please use this link to access the list:

http://www.rosenlinks.com/cea/algo

FOR FURTHER READING

Burford, Betty. *Al Gore: United States Vice President* (People to Know). Hillside, NJ: Enslow Publishers, Inc., 1994.

Fridell, Ron. *Global Warming*. New York, NY: Franklin Watts, 2002.

Gore, Al. *An Inconvenient Truth: The Crisis of Global Warming*. Rev. ed.; adapted for young readers by Jane O'Conner. New York, NY: Viking, 2007.

Harmon, Daniel E. *The Environmental Protection Agency* (Your Government: How It Works). Philadelphia, PA: Chelsea House Publishers, 2002.

Kramer, Barbara. *Tipper Gore: Activist, Author, Photographer* (People to Know). Springfield, NJ: Enslow Publishers, Inc., 1999.

Maslin, Mark. *Global Warning: Causes, Effects, and the Future*. Stillwater, MN: Voyageur Press, Inc., 2002.

BIBLIOGRAPHY

Borenstein, Seth, and Lisa Leff. "Gore's Work on Climate Earns Nobel Prize." Associated Press. *Herald-Journal* (Spartanburg, SC), October 13, 2007.

Chandler, David L. "Global Shades." *NewScientist*, July 21–27, 2007, pp. 42–45.

Drew, Lisa W. "Herd in a Hot Spot." *National Wildlife*, April/May 2007, pp. 44–50.

Dupree, Joe. "Coral Crisis." *National Wildlife*, June/July 2007, pp. 22–40.

Flannery, Tim. *The Weather Makers: How Man Is Changing the Climate and What It Means for Life on Earth.* New York, NY: Atlantic Monthly Press, 2005.

Ford, James. "On the Frontline of Climate Change: How the Inuit of the Canadian Arctic Are Weathering the Challenges of a Warmer World." *Weatherwise*, July/August 2007, pp. 42–49.

Freedman, Andrew. "Anatomy of a Forecast: Arborgeddon Takes Buffalo by Surprise." *Weatherwise*, July/August 2007, pp. 16–21.

Gelbspan, Ross. *Boiling Point.* New York, NY: Basic Books, 2004.

Gore, Al. *The Assault on Reason.* New York, NY: The Penguin Press, 2007.

Gore, Al. *Earth in the Balance: Ecology and the Human Spirit.* New York, NY: Houghton Mifflin Company, 1992.

Gore, Al. *An Inconvenient Truth: The Planetary Emergency of Global Warming and What We Can Do About It.* New York, NY: Rodale, Inc., 2006.

Grover, Ron. "Al Gore's TV Power Play." *BusinessWeek* "Power Lunch," September 18, 2007. Retrieved September 20, 2007 (http://www.businessweek.com/bwdaily/dnflash/content/sep2007/db20070918_162206.htm).

Hart, John. "Global Warming." *Microsoft Encarta 2006.* Redmond, WA: Microsoft Corporation, 2005.

An Inconvenient Truth: A Global Warning. DVD. Directed by Davis Guggenheim. Los Angeles, CA: Paramount Home Entertainment, 2006.

Maraniss, David, and Ellen Nakashima. *The Prince of Tennessee: The Rise of Al Gore.* New York, NY: Simon & Schuster, 2000.

McCaffrey, Paul, ed. *Global Climate Change* (The Reference Shelf). New York, NY: The H. W. Wilson Company, 2006.

Milius, Susan. "Den Mothers: Bears Shift Dens as Ice Deteriorates." *Science News*, July 21, 2007, p. 37.

Moynihan, Michael C. "Free Speech for People Who Think Like Me." Reasononline. June 12, 2007. Retrieved October 4, 2007 (http://reason.com/news/show/120701.html).

Perkins, Sid. "What Goes Up: Big-City Air Pollution Moves to the Burbs and Beyond." *Science News*, September 8, 2007, pp. 152–153, 156.

Pooley, Eric. "The Last Temptation of Al Gore." *Time*, May 16, 2007. Retrieved October 4, 2007 (http://www.time.com/time/nation/article/0,8599,1622009,00.html).

Richtel, Matt. "Investment Firm Names Gore as a Partner." *New York Times,* November 13, 2007 Retrieved November 13, 2007 (http://www.nytimes.com/2007/11/13/technology/13gore.html).

Roleff, Tamara L., ed. *Global Warming* (Opposing Viewpoints). San Diego, CA: Greenhaven Press, Inc., 1997.

Svoboda, Elizabeth. "The Fuel Cell." *Popular Science*, July 2007, pp. 76–82, 99.

Tennesen, Michael. "Climbing Against Time." *National Wildlife*, April/May 2007, pp. 30a–30g.

Tumulty, Karen. "Lights, Camera, Al Gore!" *Time*, May 28, 2006. Retrieved October 4, 2007 (http://www.time.com/time/magazine/article/0,9171,1198888,00.html).

Turque, Bill. *Inventing Al Gore: A Biography*. Boston, MA: Houghton Mifflin Company, 2000.

Ulrich, Lawrence. "Green-Fuel Guide." *Popular Science*, May 2007, pp. 76–81.

Williams, Jack. "Hurricane." *Microsoft Encarta 2006*. Redmond, WA: Microsoft Corporation, 2005.

Wu, Corinna. "Cellulose Dreams: The Search for New Means and Materials for Making Ethanol." *Science News*, August 25, 2007, pp. 120–121.

Zeitchik, Steven. "Quill Book Awards Unveil Winners." *Variety*, September 10, 2007. Retrieved September 11, 2007 (http://www.variety.com/index.asp?layout=print_story&articleid="VR1117971742&categoryid=1985).

Zelnick, Bob. *Gore: A Political Life*. Washington, DC: Regnery Publishing, Inc., 1999.

INDEX

About the Author

Daniel E. Harmon is a veteran author and periodical editor and writer. His articles have appeared in dozens of national and regional magazines and newspapers. Among his more than fifty other educational books are studies of government agencies, including the U.S. Environmental Protection Agency. He lives in Spartanburg, South Carolina.

Photo Credits

Designer: Tahara Anderson; Editor: Kathy Kuhtz Campbell
Photo Researcher: Amy Feinberg